THE WAY WE LIVE
in the country

STAFFORD CLIFF

THE WAY WE LIVE

in the country

GILLES DE CHABANEIX

INTRODUCTION

Pages 1–5: The wide, open spaces of the countryside lift the spirits with their fresh air, unspoilt green expanses and sense of endless possibility: autumn in the Connecticut River Valley in western Massachusetts, USA (*page 1*); tiny villages surrounded by ancient farmland in Norfolk, England (*pages 2–3*); mist descends on the vast, winding cornfields alongside Coon Creek in Wisconsin, USA (*pages 4–5*).

Page 6: Quintessential 'country': a local herd makes its way through the back lanes of a Welsh farming community. Husbandry and cultivation are defining elements of the rural way of life.

Page 7: A signpost in Devon, England, entices the visitor onto the footpaths and country lanes.

Welcome to country-house living, French style! The narrow gateway to a medieval château in the Auvergne (*opposite*) opens out into the paved courtyard, an architectural metaphor for the attractions of a rustic lifestyle, emblematic of everything that is not town and city.

This book is a celebration of the many ways in which we choose to live in the country – in Europe, the Americas, Australia and places even further afield. It explores not only homes and interiors, but also the landscape itself, and the elements of the rural lifestyle that draw people from the town or city to the countryside.

Many years ago, long before mobile phones or sat-nav, I went to visit a friend who lived in central France. As the light began to fade, my companions and I found ourselves driving along narrow roads in open farmland with our map and our directions running out. Suddenly up ahead we noticed a narrow track leading through fields to a distant farmhouse. We knew that we had arrived at the right place because every few feet along both sides of this road my friend had placed old jam jars containing little flickering candles. The effect was heart-stopping and memorable, and it said 'Welcome' in a way no words ever could. The scene comes to mind again now, because it distils the special qualities of living in the country, or visiting those who do.

In the 1960s, when I first came to live in London, the shock of city life was alleviated for me by frequent visits to a family who lived in a converted oast house in deepest Kent. They had recently moved out of London with their two little girls, and had enthusiastically embraced all the qualities that country life had to offer, both in the way that they furnished their house, and through their participation in the local community. Every Christmas I was invited to stay for a few days, sleeping in one of the distinctive round bedrooms that had once been a hop storeroom. In winter the fires would be lit and crackling, and the smell of burning logs would mingle with the fresh spruce scent of the Christmas tree (the girls made the decorations themselves) and the heady perfume of winter-flowering narcissus. Although winter can be the harshest season in the countryside, it is also the time that defines some of its most intense pleasures: log fires, bracing walks in the wind or the snow, muddy Wellington boots, a hoar frost that lasts all day, a rainbow after the rain – things so evocative of country life that they have almost become clichés.

Although country living may be synonymous with hospitality, friendship and sharing, there are many pleasures of country life that do not involve entertaining or house parties: the peace and the quiet, for instance, and the light. Whatever the countryside you are familiar with, you will enjoy the special quality of light that comes from the big skies – especially at night. Whether you are in Scandinavia, the Mediterranean, the American Midwest or the Australian Mid North, the light and the air of the countryside will have an almost magical effect on your spirit, an experience that city folk only read about.

In the past, most country-dwellers were born in their communities and rarely left them, sharing both the pleasures of country life and the hardships, of which there were many. But nowadays there are two types of country folk. There are those who were born there, as I was, and still make a living from the land, working with the changes of weather and the ebb and flow of the seasons. Then there are those who buy a house in the country at some point in their lives when funds and lifestyle allow, adopting a country base either temporarily or permanently, as my friends did. In recent years there has been an increase in this trend, as people move out of town in search of a better way of life or a different, more satisfying source of income. Finally there is the third element in the equation: children. Many parents decide on a move to the countryside when their children are young, so they can have all the advantages of a rural upbringing (although the children may long for a few more city diversions when they reach their teens).

In some cases a country house may be close enough for the owner to commute daily to a city job; others use their country house for holiday and weekend retreats. The benefits and drawbacks of this urban influx have been the topic of much debate: do the newcomers make a positive contribution to country life or do they only undermine local resources? People who only come on Friday nights and leave on Sunday afternoons don't need a post office, a library or a local school, but they do encourage farm shops and local producers, craftsmen, builders and handymen, and have also been responsible for the increase in good country restaurants and better food in pubs and hotels.

In Britain the term 'country house' denotes a particular style: the stately home, still surviving as a reminder of the extravagant lifestyles once enjoyed by wealthy aristocratic landowners. The majority of these homes are now run by the National Trust and open to the public, or have been converted into luxurious flats or country hotels. In France, there are the châteaux; in the American South, the plantation houses. Worldwide, there are many other distictive country house styles that vary from region to region and country to country, depending on local traditions and the supply of building materials.

Overleaf: In rolling California countryside, not far from the urban intensity of San Francisco, this garden seems at one with the surrounding landscape. Even the garden furniture, engagingly rustic, suggests that the human impact has been engineered with a sympathetic eye to the farmland beyond.

Some of the best domestic architecture is found in the countryside, where space is generally less restricted and suitability to weather and location are guiding factors. Builders must take into account the direction of the rains, the prevailing winds, the path of the sun and the available views. The footprint of the building is important too: is the house on one level or two? A long, thin layout, a T-shape, a U-shape, or a square, perhaps with a protected inner courtyard? Whatever it is built from – brick, stone, wood, straw or mud – the overall effect of a country house will be mellow, timeless and sympathetic to the environment, perhaps made from materials that will one day sink back into the earth. Not all country houses are traditional buildings, family homes unchanged for generations. Many have been converted, adapted, extended or modernized from existing structures. At the opposite extreme are modern houses in country settings, featuring contemporary architecture, new technologies such as solar energy and building materials with a low carbon footprint. Some feel that these houses threaten the traditional styles of country living; others find them a thrilling contrast.

The country town or village faces a similar dilemma: should it preserve traditional ways of life at any cost, or adapt to change and become like every other high street up and down the land in the process. Certainly we are drawn to towns or villages that have retained their old-fashioned charm, but we still want to buy modern products. Opinions vary, but one thing is for certain: the countryside must never be trapped in a time-warp, regarded as a theme park or folklore museum. The countryside is, as it has always been, a place full of life, whatever shape that life may take.

This book is not only about location. Country life is also a state of mind: you don't have to live in the country to have a country kitchen or to enjoy country cooking. In fact, the country kitchen – a timeless embodiment of a casual, unpretentious, family-based way of life – has captured the imagination of people all over the world, and sits in harmony with even the most modern interior design styles, from townhouse chic to hi-tech. But country-style interiors involve more than décor, as you will see in the following pages. There is a simplicity and a robust fitness for purpose that infuses every element: the style of furniture, the choices of wall and floor finishes, the window treatments and light-fittings, down to the smallest details such as door handles and crockery. As in a traditional farmhouse recipe, the ingredients for living in the country are timeless good taste, generous proportions and above all, practicality and comfort.

Stafford Cliff

These pages: One of the major attractions of life in the country is the possibility of enjoying unfettered views of superb landscapes. The mere act of setting table and chairs outside creates a relationship with the surrounding natural world. These two examples – one in southern France (*above*), the other beside the Hudson River in New York State (*opposite*) – beautifully evoke the benefits of leaving behind urban chaos and sprawl.

Following pages: The sweeping white
forms of these 'butterfly' chairs make
a dramatic sculptural group in an
open garden of a Tuscan country
house. The backdrop to this airy,
expansive area for a social gathering
is the classic landscape of Tuscany,
beloved of poets and painters, its
hills studded with the tall forms of
cypress trees.

COUNTRY LANDSCAPES

One of the prime considerations in choosing a country residence over a town or city dwelling is the landscape itself. This may be flat, hilly, mountainous, pastoral or wooded, but whatever its dominant characteristics, one thing is certain: it will be alive, both in the ways it has evolved over the ages and in the variety of colour brought by the changing seasons. Many of the clusters of houses, churches and buildings on these pages seem to have grown organically over the years to the point where they form part of the landscape itself. Buying an existing country house, or constructing a new one, will also depend on its proximity to local facilities. Few people can live happily in total isolation or would want to do without the joys of the produce available at country markets. The small towns and villages illustrated on the following pages clearly provide the necessary infrastructure for the country dweller: small shops, local foods and the all-important market stall.

A window on the countryside frames the great outdoors: the enticing view from a Welsh farmhouse (*opposite*).

The edge of eastern European wildernesses in Slovakia (*above*) and Romania (*opposite*); these landscape views indicate minimal human intervention, and in their scope evoke the essence of the rural, of everything that takes us away from town and city.

These landscape views (*opposite*), drawn from a number of European countries, including France (*top left*), Spain (*top right*), Slovakia (*below left*) and Greece (*below right*), powerfully evoke the variety of effects that the countryside and rural lifestyle can elicit in us as human intruders who go to such places to experience everything that is the antithesis of urban.

Viewed close up, the rural environment can appear distinctly welcoming after even minimal human intervention: a narrow avenue leads to a village in northern Mallorca (*right*).

Perhaps nothing symbolizes our efforts to inhabit and control the landscape more than the country lane or road: seemingly an organic part of the surrounding land, but also a clear sign of the joys of being in the country, from Mauritius (*top left, top right and bottom right*) to the Cotswolds (*upper centre right*), France (*upper centre left and bottom left*), New York State (*lower centre right*) and Sweden (*lower centre left*).

Nowhere is the country road more important than in the vastness of Australia (*right*), where it is a crucial means of connecting the country's far-flung communities through rain or shine, drought or flood.

The human imprint on the
landscape varies in its intensity, from
a simple country road (in Romania,
above) to whole cities, for instance
Tuscan Siena (*opposite*). Even such
an urban centre can appear at one
with the surrounding countryside,
as though it had grown directly out
of it. Siena's venerable buildings rise
up suddenly from cultivated fields
and vineyards.

This quality of belonging to the land, however, is usually felt much more deeply in small towns and villages: in the French Alps (*left above*), and in a straggling hillside village in Corsica (*left below*).

Often perched near the summit of hills, presumably for protection, are the renowned 'white villages' of Andalucia (*right above and below*). Their narrow alleys and streets, ancient monuments and Moorish ruins provide a relief for country-dwellers in an often heat-drenched landscape.

The 'street', sometimes deserted in the afternoon sun, as in this scene from southern Portugal (*left above*), or a bustling centre of local life, as here in Cartagena, Colombia (*left below*), is a vital artery of the rural community where, depending on the time of day and the weather, residents of a village or a neighbourhood can socialize, shop or gossip.

This page: Such 'main streets' are repeated endlessly in different forms throughout the world: a single thoroughfare drawing together the various elements of small-town life, whether in Hamley Bridge in South Australia (*right above*) or in Saratoga Springs in upstate New York (*right below*).

Following pages: Newly valued in the age of shopping mall and hypermarket, the small country shop has almost attained the revered status of a folk-art. Examples from Ireland (*top left, centre left and centre right*), Wales (*top right*), Spain (*below left*) and India (*below right*) all exhibit an air of inviting intimacy as they make their special contributions to the local social fabric (*page 32*). Though less well-appointed than the country shop, the road-side stall serves a similar function all over the world, from Guatemala to Madagascar and beyond (*page 33*).

From Provence (*opposite*) to Nepal (*right*), the local market provides all the good things of country living, and immediate contact with the agricultural world. The imagery of the market stall, however simple, is rich in colour, texture, form and pattern, brought together in an alluring display of freshness. It is another element of the response to the perennial question: why would we like to live in the country?

A country market should be a place of abundance and conviviality, both characteristics of many of the weekly markets in the villages and towns of southern France (*left and opposite*). Elizabeth David and M. F. K. Fisher, almost certainly the greatest writers in English on the culinary arts, found a unique joy in the sheer volume and variety of seasonal produce on offer in a good market in the Mediterranean region: tomatoes, courgettes, peppers, melons, asparagus, strawberries, redcurrants, cherries, apricots, peaches, pears and plums.

A sight often seen in the villages and small towns of the French Midi is a market composed of open-sided vans, sometimes mixed with conventional market stalls (*opposite and right*). The 'van' stalls are used especially for the sale of fresh meat, fish and cheese.

First steps in the harvesting of fresh foodstuffs from the kitchen garden (*left and opposite*): how attractive the produce of the country can look, a world apart from the supply chains that lead to the food-processing plant and the supermarket!

The traditional country dwelling,
like these two stone-built Mallorcan
houses (*above and opposite*),
is usually surrounded by ample
outdoor space to be colonized and
cultivated. The owners of one house
(*above*) have chosen to emphasize
the colours of the local earth and
rocks, surrounding the building with
an arrangement of cacti and stone.

In contrast, another house in the
same region (*above*) sits happily near
its verdant kitchen garden, a place of
obviously flourishing produce.

A strictly formal approach to the planning and planting of the country garden can create a scene of dramatic contrast to the surrounding countryside, forming an elaborate extension of living areas. Such a vision was at the heart of the great horticultural confections of seventeenth-century France, a tradition repeated in these contemporary country gardens in Charente (*left above and below*) and in southern France (*opposite*).

A cultivated garden with a glimpse of the landscape beyond: scenes such as these must surely represent the essence of country living for most people. Dappled light falls upon a profusion of plant life around a house in the Auvergne region of France (*left above*), and at an English farmhouse in Charleston, Sussex (*left below*), made famous by the occupancy of writers and artists from the Bloomsbury Group, including Vanessa Bell and Duncan Grant.

Although both are somewhat formal, these two country gardens – one French (*right above*) and one Spanish (*right below*) – blend remarkably well with everything around them, not only their immediate surrounding vegetation, but also the more distant landscape. The presence of an impromtu dining area in the French garden creates a wonderful spectacle of country living, a vision enhanced by trees and borders in combination with old iron gates and weathered masonry.

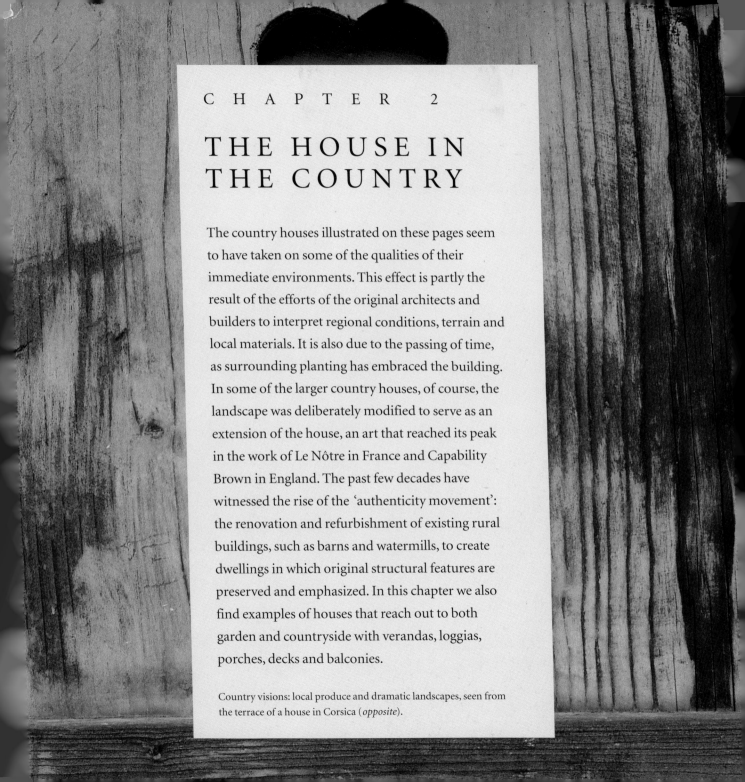

CHAPTER 2

THE HOUSE IN THE COUNTRY

The country houses illustrated on these pages seem to have taken on some of the qualities of their immediate environments. This effect is partly the result of the efforts of the original architects and builders to interpret regional conditions, terrain and local materials. It is also due to the passing of time, as surrounding planting has embraced the building. In some of the larger country houses, of course, the landscape was deliberately modified to serve as an extension of the house, an art that reached its peak in the work of Le Nôtre in France and Capability Brown in England. The past few decades have witnessed the rise of the 'authenticity movement': the renovation and refurbishment of existing rural buildings, such as barns and watermills, to create dwellings in which original structural features are preserved and emphasized. In this chapter we also find examples of houses that reach out to both garden and countryside with verandas, loggias, porches, decks and balconies.

Country visions: local produce and dramatic landscapes, seen from the terrace of a house in Corsica (*opposite*).

A farmhouse in Menorca typifies the contemporary liking for a back-to-the-country approach to living, whereby the restoration of run-down or previously abandoned buildings is preferred to new construction.

Isolation is sometimes sought for specific reasons, as in the case of this Scottish hunting lodge (*left*). A renovated hill-top farmhouse in Tuscany, surrounded by cypress trees (*left below*), suggests the realization of a quest for rural peace and quiet.

This more recent construction in South Australia (*right above*), encircled by fully grown trees, repeats the theme of deliberate rural isolation, as does the Menorcan farmhouse surrounded by its fortress of pines (*right below*).

Country living on the grand scale: a hunting lodge sits majestically in a mountainous winter landscape near Salzburg, Austria (*left*), a dominant presence in dramatic surroundings. In an earlier era, this medieval castle in Ireland (*opposite*) would have been a symbol of human control over the land around it. Now, partially restored and refurbished, it makes a remarkable country residence.

The houses we choose as our living or lodging places relate in very different ways to their rural settings, but all the examples on these pages do have an air of being entirely appropriate to what surrounds them. This fishing lodge by a Scottish loch (*opposite*), for instance, is almost certainly built of local materials. A simple cabin in Central Australia (*right above*) has a simplicity that reflects the drama and traditions of the land on which it is built, while the elegance of this villa just outside Cairo (*right below*) is an expression of the highly sophisticated lifestyle of Egypt's social elite.

Choosing a place to live in the country, especially if that place is isolated and in need of substantial restoration and upkeep, as is the case with these examples (*left*), is very much a matter of personal taste and means. All these homes have great individuality, and – whether on the plain or in the mountains – each leaves a distinctive human imprint on the countryside. The refurbishment of such buildings always holds certain challenges, which should be set against the possibility of creating dwellings of unique magnificence, as would this stone tower in the Greek mountains, were it to be restored sympathetically (*opposite*).

The formal dwellings illustrated here (*this page and opposite*) reflect the high status of the owners of the surrounding land and conceivably also of the parkland beyond. In regional styles ranging from classical French (*left above*) and Gustavian Swedish (*opposite above*), to colonial upstate New York (*left below*) and Moorish resonances in a former private chapel in Menorca (*opposite below*), they exemplify distinctive forms of refined country architecture.

Contrasts in country living styles: substantial houses in Austria (*top left and right*), Canada (*upper centre left and right*), the English Cotswolds (*lower centre left*), southern France (*lower centre right and bottom right*) and New York State (*bottom left*) continue the theme of rural life pursued in some luxury. A very different approach is evoked by this simple, modest cottage in Wales (*opposite*), surrounded by a magnificent traditional country garden.

A relaxed rural architectural style, appropriate to a new and vibrant nation: these Australian country houses, though in different states, all have an openness of aspect and easy access to the surrounding gardens. This sense of being part of the immediate environment is accentuated by the extensive use of verandas, at once part of the house, but also part of the garden: in South Australia (*left above and below*), in Victoria (*opposite above*) and in the hills near Adelaide (*opposite below*).

Decorative elements frequently appear in the form of intricate cast-iron work, a feature of both rural and urban architecture in Australia. Much of this kind of embellishment was bought prefabricated from British manufacturers' catalogues.

Now preserved as part of a folk museum near Salzburg, these traditional Austrian farmhouses (*left and opposite*) are fine representations of one response to the rigours of living in the country. Shuttered lower windows would have protected the occupants from wind and drifting snow during the Alpine winters, while the long, elaborately carved galleries permitted views above the snow line.

The flamboyance of decoration in the farmhouses of Bohemia is striking (*opposite and right*). During the the eighteenth and nineteenth centuries even the most humble country buildings in the region began to display a richness of design on their façades and gateways. The distinctive painted reliefs were often executed in a vaguely Baroque style, echoing the architecture of the great cities and towns nearby.

Undoubtedly one of the pleasures of taking over a traditional house in the country is the preservation of its original fabric and texture, which varies widely by region (*left*). Restoration may be desirable, or indeed necessary, but the retention and preservation of the well-worn material of the structure adds enormously to its attraction and provides an even more cogent reason for maintaining elements that are expressive of the indigenous architecture, such as the deep plastered window-niches in this traditional stone house in Menorca (*opposite*).

In contrast to the structural detail illustrated on the preceding pages, these façades in New York State (*above left*), France (*above right*), Canada (*opposite left*) and Chile (*opposite right*) signal a more formal and calculated approach to country living. Like the veranda, the front porch is an area of transition between house and garden, a place from which surrounding land may be contemplated while still retaining some proximity to the pleasures of life inside the home.

These pages: Timber construction for village and country homes reached a kind of perfection in the clapboard houses of New England. Classical in proportion with porticoes in a variety of styles (*left and opposite*), these dwellings traditionally had a reputation for openness to the local community, here symbolized by touches such as lucky horseshoes on the stoop and benches just outside the front door.

Overleaf: For those dreaming of an alternative existence outside the city, one of the most alluring images must be that of dining alfresco. In this example, the benevolent climate and light of the Mediterranean afford the owners of a traditional dwelling on the island of Ibiza the opportunity to have candlelit dinners out in the open.

These pages and overleaf: Different countries, different locations, but all are united in the pursuit of culinary pleasures in country gardens. These scenes suggest copious amounts of sunlight, the prospect of good local food and a generally relaxed lifestyle, whether in a home in Corsica (*left above*) or in Provence (*opposite above and overleaf*). In two gardens in upstate New York (*left below and opposite below*) the planting has created a growth of foliage that enhances the intimacy of the dining area.

In all these gardens the presence of shrubs and trees is vital to the creation of a pleasant spot for the enjoyment of food, drink and the company of friends. The slightly haphazard quality of these outdoor environments is in profound contrast to the formality of the town garden or terrace.

CHAPTER 3

TRADITIONAL HOMES

Some are modest, some grand, and some specially created to evoke the rural life of times gone by, but all the interiors illustrated in this chapter in some way express distinctively traditional ways of approaching life in the country. There are large houses, furnished for maximum comfort with chairs and sofas gathered around magnificent open fireplaces, and entrance halls that offer an immediate welcome after walks on country paths and lanes. Here, too, are small kitchens and dining rooms whose decoration and even utensils and equipment suggest a rustic existence. Many of these interiors, whether of substantial houses or of more modest cottages, make a special feature of the original structure of the building, leaving aged wood and rough-hewn beams exposed, bringing to the fore the special qualities of 'the house in the country'.

An English classic: the country garden beyond the windows of Charleston, the Sussex farmhouse beloved by the writers and artists of the Bloomsbury Group (*opposite*).

Preceding pages: In the country residence of a Parisian interior designer in southern France, the play of light from the surrounding garden is given greater subtlety by the hanging of light, white curtains over an arched stone entrance originally designed to admit a horse and carriage.

These pages: Entrances and exits are among the most intriguing features of any house, especially when the contrast between interior and exterior emphasizes the division between the domestic sphere and the surrounding countryside. This massive opening in the back wall of a Provençal house (*left*) takes in both the formality of the garden and the landscape backdrop, in a way adding an extra room the house. Less expansive, but no less intriguing, is an enclosed passage in another Provençal house (*opposite*), made interesting by the surrounding woodwork and the well-preserved stone floor.

Passages and corridors, those transitional areas within the home, are notoriously difficult to decorate and design. In these two instances, however – both in Spanish country homes – these confined spaces have been turned into places of daring visual delight. One example (*left*) is dominated by a superb Anatolian kilim, set off by planters on a traditional splay-legged table.

In another example, on the island of Ibiza, imaginative use has been made of the original wall to create a multi-object tableau (*right*).

Allowing the special light of the countryside into the often windowless hallways of traditional homes is always a challenge, and these four examples from around the world show how varied and imaginative the solutions can be. Entrance hallways in country houses in Goa (*above left*), Ireland (*above right*), Menorca (*opposite left*), and upstate New York (also remarkable for the painted tile effect on its original floorboards) (*opposite right*) successfully convey the promise of the sunny gardens and light-drenched vistas that lie beyond their doors.

The grander the country house, the
more impressive its entrance halls,
corridors and staircases (*above*).
Despite the spaciousness afforded
by such rural opulence, there can still
be room for the clutter necessary to
country living when the weather is
less than kindly: waterproofs, gum-
boots, umbrellas and childrens' toys
are welcome (*opposite*).

A more modest response to the decorative demands of country living typified by these two rustic interiors: in a family house near Charente (*left above and below*), and in a rural Canadian interior, notable for its wealth of contrasting woods (*opposite*).

Arranged beneath heavily beamed ceilings, these two French interiors – one near Grenoble (*above*) and one in the Auvergne region (*opposite*) – display an entirely pleasing eclecticism in their old-fashioned furniture and furnishings. Comfort and user-friendliness have clearly been uppermost in the owners' minds, providing a welcoming domestic environment in the midst of the rigours that the countryside may hold.

The furnishings of this Spanish country house (*left*) suggest a certain level of opulence in the lifestyle of its owners. A glance at the beamed ceiling, however, reveals the building's distinctly rustic past, belied by the fine furniture and rugs that the house contains.

Although there is an elegance and sophistication to the colour schemes used in the interior of this Corsican house (*right*), it is apparent from the visible presence of various structural elements that the dwelling had a much less cosseted past, suggesting conversion from a barn or a primitive farmhouse.

Preceding pages: The large country house or château clearly offers a very different version of rural living to that of the converted barn, farmhouse or country cottage. This castle in Sweden is now a folk museum, but the scale of its interiors still suggests the extravagent lifestyle that its original owners would have led.

This page: A cheerful eclecticism characterizes the interior decoration of the château of Outrelaise in Normandy (*above*). The furniture is a mix of styles: hybrid Louis-Quinze and Louis-Seize, Second Empire in the Louis-Treize manner, and nineteenth-century ease in the form of two capacious wing armchairs. Anatolian kilims enliven the floor.

This Swedish dining room (*above*), characterized by a coolly reticent northern classicism, is now preserved as a museum exhibit, but still convincingly recalls the way in which a landowner might have celebrated Christmas. The festive nature of this arrangement is indicated by the flowers sprinkled over the floor.

Kitchen areas of country homes
usually offer a more spacious
environment for food preparation
than the compressed galley designs
in many city apartments. Both
these examples, one Spanish (*above*)
and one Californian (*opposite*),
also serve as simple dining rooms,
made agreeable by the homely, rustic
nature of the decoration and fittings.

In country kitchens (*opposite*), the use of quite modest, even frugal, shelves and cupboards can seem more appropriate than expensive cabinetry, as it acknowledges the continuing traditions of the past.

Crockery, glassware and all kinds of cooking utensils can make a marvellous display against the strong, earthy colours of these interiors. Vibrant warm-toned yellows add light and life to the cottage kitchen, as in this Corsican home (*right*).

Although the re-creation in folk museums of lives gone by highlights significant differences compared to the décor and organization of present-day country homes, there are also many elements in common, such as the importance of the fireplace, the choice and display of traditional furniture and treasured possessions – plates, vases and rural implements. In a Swedish reconstruction (*left*) a corner fireplace dominates the room; in a Welsh example (*opposite*) a fine wheel-back Windsor chair faces the traditional coal-fired cooking range.

Preceding pages: A Provençal dining room *par excellence*: traditional ladderback dining chairs surround a simple wooden table. The raised fireplace suggests that it was once used for cooking. Beneath the window a collection of terracotta storage jars displays the earthy yellows and greens so strongly associated with the textiles and crockery of the region.

A mixture of the re-created and the absolutely contemporary, all sharing an authentic rustic quality: these are family environments embodying the essence of country living. In a Swedish folk museum (*opposite left*) and in a preserved traditional farmhouse in upstate New York (*opposite right*) great pains have been taken to reconstruct the details of nineteenth-century life in rural communities. The essential elements of these two settings remain in two present-day country houses, one in France (*above left*), and the other in Sicily (*above right*), where traditional refectory tables provide additional space for food preparation.

Simple, but pre-eminently places of ease: kitchens and dining rooms in a Mediterranean setting (*above*) and in a country house near the coast of Chile (*opposite*). All the features and furnishings, from fireplace to dining table, suggest functionality and rural hardiness.

These scenes, from country houses in the south of France (*left above, opposite above and opposite below*) and in upstate New York (*left below*), suggest a more sophisticated approach to country living than the rustic examples illustrated on the preceding pages.

Though still distinctly 'country', these interiors suggest that the owners have wanted to create very fine living spaces, albeit in a rural environment. Some of the furniture, for instance, would look entirely at home in an elegant townhouse.

Certain interior features inevitably evoke rural living: white plaster walls, unpainted woodwork, exposed roofbeams and unadorned windows, for instance. Simple flooring tiles – very different from their elaborately cut and coloured urban cousins – in a converted farmhouse in Tuscany (*above left*), a French farmhouse in the Cévennes (*opposite left*), and in a distinctively Provençal dwelling (*opposite right*), always convey the suggestion that the great outdoors is not far away.

There is always something special about dining in the place where food is prepared. This kitchen (*right*), clearly rustic yet classically elegant, is used in exactly the same way as it was in the late eighteenth century, when the house it serves was built in upstate New York. The walls have been painted in the colours of the period, and the fireplace restored to its original function as a cooking range.

The installations in the folk museum of Skansen, near Stockholm, contain many objects and decorative features that re-create rural life in the pre-plastics age (*left*). This wall surface may have been intended to imitate marbling, but the use of a quick-dry distemper porbably worked against the realization of any subtle effects. A truckle bed protrudes from beneath the table, suggesting a room with several uses, as does the storage of hard biscuits on poles hung just beneath the ceiling. A very rustic version of the traditional long-case clock indicates a home of some standing in spite of the simplicity of the furniture. There is a similar severity about this room in a Canadian folk museum near Quebec City (*opposite*), in spite of the massive presence of the stove, evoking the northern aesthetic also noted in Scandinavian and Scottish interiors.

Birchwood dominates as the material for the furniture in a dining-room ensemble at a folk museum in the Adirondack region of New York State (*left above*). The interior re-creates the rustic qualities that generations of New Yorkers sought when they took their summer vacations amid lakes and mountains, far away from the hot city summers. In another location in New York State, the dining room in a carefully restored house (*left below*) displays a more refined, European-style response to country living.

The sitting room of this Georgian-style house in upstate New York is painted in the pale green of its original decorative scheme (*right above*), reflecting the owner's goal of keeping the rooms as close to their late eighteenth-century appearance as possible (note also the kitchen of the same house on pages 120–21). A similar effort to pursue an elegant lifestyle in a country setting is realized successfully in the dining room of a house in southern France (*right below*).

Town or country, one of the major elements of visual drama in any home is the transition from one living area to another, from room to room and from exterior to interior. The open or half-open door leads the eye to the spaces beyond. All four of these rooms are in country houses in Provence; as is typical of the traditional local style, their uncovered floors continue uninterrupted from one room to another. The doorways – sometimes framed, sometimes not – are simply treated, with little decoration and the natural colour of the building materials predominating.

The warmth of wood: this space immediately beneath the roof of a house near Carpentras, the melon capital of Provence, provides a neat guest bedroom (*left*), perhaps for some city-dweller in need of a restorative country break.

Some of this birch furniture was originally made for a hotel in the Adirondacks that catered for vacationing New Yorkers (*opposite*). Now in a folk museum at Blue Mountain Lake, New York State, it gives a good impression of the city-dwellers' fondness for the trappings of rustic mountain life, complete with a decorative pair of snowshoes.

These pages: How fundamental is wood to the country-house bedroom, a perfect accompaniment to the soft furnishing, especially when well aged: here in houses in Provence (*above left*) and in Tuscany (*above right*). The use of wood in a chalet in the French Alps (*opposite left*) provides a more clean and contemporary look, creating a pleasantly protected and enclosed feeling in a bedroom. Somewhat more spectacular in effect is this nineteenth-century bedroom preserved in a Canadian folk museum (*opposite right*).

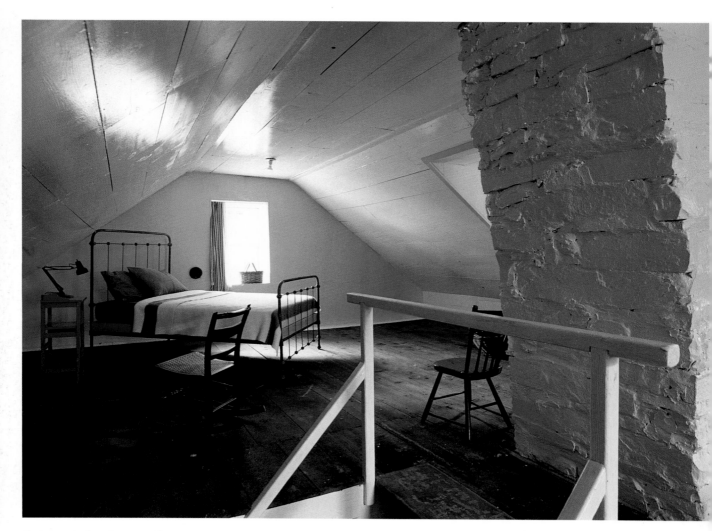

Bedrooms in the attic rooms of
old country houses, such as these
two examples in New York State
(*above and opposite*), frequently
convey a sense of enclosure, inviting
hibernation. Their furnishings, too,
often display a simplicity and lack
of finish that emphasizes their
separateness from the grander
rooms below.

The exposed beams of an old
country house put us in direct
contact with the structural
fundamentals of the building,
especially on the attic or loft floors.
There is also a secretive, hideaway
quality about cavities immediately
below the roof, picturesquely
expressed in this bedroom
(*right*) of a house in the Allier
département in central France.

All these bedrooms, decorated in the colours and styles of their original designs, are in country houses in New York State. A locally made early nineteenth-century bed dominates the master bedroom of a house of the same era (*left above*); a rag rug continues the period theme.

The elegance of these two bedrooms (*left below and opposite above*) reflects their role as the main sleeping accommodation in a fine estate house looking out towards the Hudson River. The yellow bedroom (*left below*) contains an interesting scroll-end bed, showing distinct French influence; in the nineteenth century, several French firms of cabinet-makers established themselves in New York, where they influenced local craftsmen.

The blue bedroom in the same house is furnished with more distinctively rustic pieces, some painted (*right above*). One of the guest bedrooms in this house on Long Island (*right below*) shares the generally pale colours of all the other rooms; an early nineteenth-century Pennsylvanian coverlet provides a striking note of colour.

Country-house bedrooms can also be areas for gracious living, especially through the choice of fine furniture and close attention to arrangements of objects, perhaps very personal, pleasing and distinctive, making the most of rooms in which we probably spend more time than we realize. Three of these examples are drawn from the same French country house (*above left and right*, *opposite left*). Even the stencilled floor of a bedroom in a house in upstate New York (*opposite right*) adds a grace-note to an otherwise simple setting.

An early nineteenth-century Spanish bed graces the guest bedroom in this mid eighteenth-century house in upstate New York (*left*). The original canopy has been lifted from the bedposts and fastened to the ceiling.

In a Mallorcan holiday home the children's bedroom contains a remarkable ex-convent bed, stylishly made of iron and brass (*right*).

Guest bedrooms with style in country houses in New York State: antique quilts, almost certainly made in the region, provide dramatic dashes of colour on the traditional beds (*left above and below*).

Two versions of tranquility in the bedroom: a guest room in the same Mallorcan holiday home shown on page 141 provides a restrained setting for two nineteenth-century painted iron beds (*right above*); an unrestored blue wash on the walls of the guest room in a country house in southern France creates a cool, shadowy retreat from the bright light and heat outside, and hints at the past life of the room (*right below*).

Hanging curtains from a central tester is one way of creating warmth and intimacy around a bed: an elaborate day-bed in a Provençal house (*left above*) and a much simpler Swedish example, re-created in the folk museum of Skansen (*left below*). This bedchamber of the Gustavian period would probably also have served as a sitting room, with the bed being pushed back against the wall and partly concealed by the long drapes. Total concealment of the bed is possible in this Provençal bedroom (*opposite*), creating a room that can also serve other purposes.

The free-standing bath, whether a classic claw-foot or a modern boat-shaped version, looks completely at home in the country bathroom – a fact recognized by the owners of these houses in Ibiza (*above left*), in the French Alps (*above right*) and in Provence (*opposite left and opposite right*).

Rough, untreated surfaces characterize all the rooms of this converted Mallorcan farmhouse, but none more so than the bathroom (*opposite*), illuminated by small windows let into the walls and made of slightly opaque glass to filter the strong sunlight. In the prevailing hot climate, such simplicity and lack of finish and ornament seem entirely appropriate. Similarly, this Provençal bathroom (*right*) has retained its original, straightforward fittings – brass taps and a shallow washbasin – against a background of the region's traditional ochre paint. A few personal bibelots add the only decorative note.

CHAPTER 4

CONTEMPORARY HOMES

In the preceding chapters we have looked at country homes of a certain age, characterized by the patinas of passing years and displaying distinctly traditional elements of rural living. But this is not the whole picture of the way we live outside of our urban communities. The following pages illustrate ways in which an entirely contemporary aesthetic can support the country lifestyle. Of immediate note is the use of a predominantly light palette: white or near-white walls reflect the changing quality and intensity of the natural light. This effect can be applied to older buildings, but it is especially striking in contemporary interiors, such as those of the modernist houses in the California foothills, where light is magnified by the impression of spaciousness produced by wide expanses of window leading on to gardens, swimming pools and the stunning outdoor views beyond.

A view over the Mallorcan countryside from a distinctly modernist viewpoint (*opposite*).

Although the buildings illustrated in this chapter include a mixture of traditional (*right*) and contemporary structures (*opposite*), their interiors all display a modernist sensibility in their responses to country living. The furniture and furnishings eschew self-consciously rustic qualities, whether the house itself has been built recently or is a restoration of an older building retaining some of the patina of age.

Although this elegant interior is in fact the hallway of a mid nineteenth-century clapboard house in the Hudson River Valley in upstate New York (*right*), it has been included in this chapter because of its spare, uncluttered appearance. Pastel colours form the background to a few choice pieces of antique furniture, and the floorboards of the hall have been painted to simulate black-and-white chequer-work tiles.

For country houses in the Mediterranean region, simple, light interiors also seem to be the most appropriate way of managing the living quarters. In these examples – from (*left to right*) Spain, Corsica, France and Sicily – the unfussy nature of the colour scheme has also been extended to the furniture and upholstery.

The probable origin of this French country residence as a barn (*right*) is apparent in the stripped vertical posts and cross-beams visible beneath a wooden ceiling. Yet, in the midst of these (well-restored) reminders of the building's rustic past, the owners have chosen furniture that would not be out of place in a city apartment. The new fireplace, too, speaks of an entirely contemporary design aesthetic. The very simplicity of all these additions makes them look entirely at home amid the elements retained from the original construction.

One of the obvious delights of country living is the scope for surrounding a home with planting, so that every view allows the occupants to experience the sensation of the natural world at close hand and to observe the changing of the colours with the seasons. Once again, white or near-white has been chosen as the dominant background colour in these two French interiors. Distinctly modern glass panels allow a whole vista of vegetation in one example (*above*), while the traditional window form, with its wooden shutters, has been retained in the other (*opposite*). Wooden furniture and rugs bring warmth and interest to both interiors.

These pages: Mediterranean sunlight outside; cool, relaxing interiors inside, this sitting room (*above*), furnished in a pleasingly eclectic way, is in one of Ibiza's traditional flat-roofed houses. Small window apertures guarantee the coolness of the interior in summer and help retain heat in winter. A similar effect is achieved in a Tunisian house featuring thick plastered walls and a curved roof and fireplace (*opposite*).

Overleaf: In a small country town in Provence, this elegant interior is obviously the result of a measured and straightforward approach to decoration. A light, airy sitting room has been unified by a monochromatic colour scheme. A relatively small number of articles of furniture complement the the décor to create a spacious, pared-down effect.

In spite of low ceilings and relatively restricted window areas, these two Provençal interiors (*above and opposite*) express the sense of freedom and relaxation inherent in country living. Light background colours combine with unfussy furniture to create contemporary room settings that are comfortable, yet entirely fitting in old rural houses.

Many of the interiors illustrated on the preceding pages make great play with light colours and tones, both in background decoration and in the furnishing of the rooms. These two interiors – in Normandy (*left above*) and California (*left below*) – use pale colours in the furniture, offsetting the deeper, warmer colours that books and other personal objects inevitably bring into a room.

In these two interiors – a Provençal house (*right above*), and a north Italian farmhouse (*right below*) – the colour white on walls and furniture looks as though it has been applied for its own intrinsic qualities, rather than as a sympathetic background. The patterned accent fabrics stand out dramatically against the understated paint scheme.

This kind of modernist structure and interior design (*right*) is particularly representative of the architectural style of California from the 1930s onwards, characterized by cool, rationally managed spaces and views – a rural American interpretation of the European aesthetic of Le Corbusier and Gropius.

Three houses in the Californian countryside (*left above and below, and opposite below*), and another in Normandy (*opposite above*) are entirely contemporary in their furnishing, with a distinct emphasis on comfort.

These four interiors all evoke traditional methods of rural building in their generous use of wood and their exposure of structural elements and surfaces.

One internal feature that always rates highly in any country house is that supreme focus of the decorator's attention, the sight of which may gladden one's being after a walk in the winter countryside: the fireplace. In all of these rooms – in houses in Normandy (*left above*) and southern France (*left below*), in an early nineteenth-century clapboard house in upstate New York (*opposite above*), and in the Provençal holiday home of a fashion designer (*opposite below*) – the whole arrangement of the interior has been directed towards the fireplace, both in the position of the furniture and in the use of the mantelpiece and chimney breast for the display of objects and paintings.

Curvaceous, round-backed
Chesterfield-style sofas accentuate
the sense of cosiness and casual
comfort in all four rooms.

These pages: Two Californian examples of rural living offer different solutions to the arrangement of dining areas, varying from modernist simplicity (*above*) to more traditional furniture: cupboards, cabinets, and a formal dining table (*opposite*). Both display the characteristic Californian large window area and still manage to make rustic references in their beamed wooden ceilings.

Overleaf: This arched dining room in an ancient house in the Apulia region of Italy (*left*) was in fact converted from a former stable. The rough-hewn stonework vaults of the same building, giving on to an internal courtyard, have been opened to create a perfect space for alfresco dining (*right*).

Spacious country houses near San Francisco (*opposite*); in upstate New York, with painted chairs (*right above*); and in southern France (*right below*) make effective use of the simplest dining arrangements. It is worth noting that the chairs, perhaps even more so than the table, create the rustic look that is exactly right for the rural setting, be it contemporary or traditional.

The interiors of a fashion designer's holiday home in a small town in Provence exude spaciousness and light (*right*). Any potential darkening effect of the low ceilings has been nullified by the overall colour scheme, in which even the ceiling beams have been included. Two long kitchen tables create a substantial dining surface for family and friends, while the metal chairs can easily be used for dining outside, if necessary.

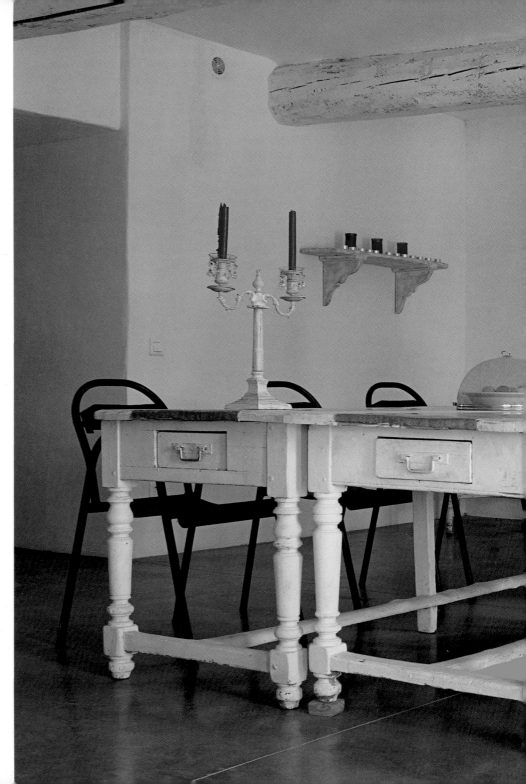

In houses on the Île de Ré in western France (*above left*), near Seville (*above right*); and in Sicily (*opposite*), these kitchen–dining rooms speak volumes for the success of the unadorned approach in furnishing a country home. They are functional yet homely; some of the furniture may very well have been bought new from mainstream stores, then combined with older pieces, which are still to be found relatively cheaply in flea markets and bric-à-brac emporiums.

Integrated kitchen–diners,
rural style, these two magnificent
cooking and eating areas, both
in Californian houses (*above
and opposite*), combine the luxury
of contemporary equipment
with certain 'country' touches,
emphasizing casual dining and
the views out to surrounding gardens.

Touches of colour enliven the dining room of this Californian house (*opposite*), with bright yellows suggesting the hues of sunlit gardens in bloom. A gap in the wall, echoed by the table runner and the hanging lamp, leads directly on to the kitchen (*right*), giving the diners an appetizing view of the well-ordered shelves of containers and jars.

The arrangements of display shelving in a house in California (*left and opposite*) offer a novel and ingenious updating of the traditional cabinets of curiosities. In both rooms, the displays – one of intriguing found objects, the other of vibrant coloured glassware – have been built around openings giving access to the surrounding garden.

In spite of the distinctly rustic appearance of its ceiling, this bedroom (*left*) is in fact part of the accommodation in a relatively modern Californian house.

The antiquity of this house
in southern France (*right*) is
immediately apparent from the
rough crossbeams and floorboards
of the loft space immediately above
the sleeping quarters.

Overleaf: This vaulted room in a
Provençal *mas*, the country home of
a French interior designer, makes a
light and airy bedroom. The rough-
cast wall surface has been carefully
cleaned, but the rugged strength
of the structure still commands
attention. Traditional Provençal
terracotta tiles form the floor.

All the bedrooms illustrated on these pages (*opposite and right*) provide sympathetic sleeping quarters in the hot climate and intense light of the Mediterranean lands, from southern France and Italy to North Africa. Almost all the owners of these rural houses have opted for a look of cool simplicity in both decoration and furnishing. There is only one note of high elaboration: the Louis-Quinze style bed (*right*).

CHAPTER 5

COUNTRY DETAILS

As with most aspects of decoration and design, it is often the finishing touches to rustic interiors and exteriors that make any scheme totally effective. Such details may include the treatment and preservation of original doors and windows, the painting of awkward spaces such as verandas, corridors and landings, and the display of personal items and found objects. Judging from the images on these pages, it is perhaps in the rural kitchen that we find the most interesting examples of country detail. Here are the unusual shapes and intriguing objects – typically those of the pre-plastic age – that embody the pleasures of rural life: crockery displayed on open shelves; utensils and containers on dressers and work surfaces and, most important of all, food fresh from the *potager*.

Attention to detail: personalized decorative elements in the deep window recess of a Provençal country home (*opposite*).

In warmer climates the loggia or veranda of a substantial country house can easily serve as an additional living room or gallery, open to the garden but still providing plenty of space for sitting or dining. Much of the summer life of this house on the Hudson River in New York State (*left above*) takes place on a magnificent colonnaded veranda opening on to a garden that sweeps down to the river itself. Similarly, the wide and accommodating loggia of a country house on the island of Mauritius (*left below*) is both part of the house (the dining room is just visible at its far end) and an extension of the garden. An array of blinds acts as a shield against strong sunlight.

The use of the veranda or loggia as an architectural device to link house and garden or courtyard is found all over the world: here, in India (*right above*) and in Spain (*right below*). This latter example runs along one side of the main residence in a seventeenth-century hacienda near Seville.

There is a sympathetic, heart-warming quality about wooden surfaces that bear the signs of age, the patina of long-time use. Doors, especially, when original to older country houses, provide a memorable record of rural life in times gone by, as in this house in northern France (*above left*), on an antique door in a Spanish home (*above right*), on a split 'Dutch' door in a restored seventeenth-century dwelling in upstate New York (*opposite left*), and a magnificently sculpted door in a country house near Prague (*opposite right*).

It's all in the details: rustic latches and handles on aged doors (*left*), including a section of branch (*below left*) and a traditional hook fastening (*below right*). Sometimes, however, country simplicity yields to more elaborate decorative devices, such as this splendid door-knocker on a cottage in a Mexican village (*opposite*), with a double row of bells that ring when the knocker is operated.

Sometimes it is the seemingly insignificant space or feature that provides the opportunity to reinforce a desired look. Hallways and external doors, for instance, can easily be the focus of decorative detail, emphasizing the 'country' aspect of a house, as in this hallway in Provence (*opposite*), and the restored screen door of a house in upstate New York (*right*).

Passages, corridors, staircases and landings are the main areas of transition within the home. They are always a challenge to the decorator but, successfully treated, are crucial to conveying the 'feel' of any house. Washed-out blues, for instance, on the doors of this bedroom hallway reflect the late eighteenth-century origins of a restored house on Long Island (*left*). The floor rugs re-create traditional patterns. Past patinas have been retained everywhere in the corridors and rooms of this old Provençal house (*opposite*), avoiding any intrusive restoration and redecoration.

Careful finish and attention to detail characterize these hallways, which are also notable for their sympathetic, harmonious application of colour – nothing jars. In each case, furniture has been deployed sparingly, but with an eye to creating points of subtle interest: a house in upstate New York painted in authentic nineteenth-century colours (*above left*); panelled shutters in an Umbrian farmhouse (*above right*); the capacious entrance hall of a Provençal house (*opposite left*) and buttermilk décor and an antique hanging birdcage in a Corsican house (*opposite right*).

These two staircases have been made features of interest in their respective houses, providing arresting shapes in their own right, as well as additional display areas for objects and furniture. In a house in Long Island, New York, antique tables and chairs are placed in eye-catching positions (*left*). Beside the original staircase in a house in Charente (*opposite*) an antique chest provides a surface for the owner's collection of local pottery.

The importance of the transition from one living area to another can scarcely be overstated in terms of the overall decoration of a house. Visual drama in any home is often created by the open or half-open door leading the eye to whatever lies beyond it. In these country houses – in northern Italy (*above left*); in Greece (*above right*); in Goa (*opposite left*) and on the island of Ibiza (*opposite right*) – various solutions for outlining a doorway or replacing a traditional doorframe have been employed by their respective owners.

On the inside looking out: the windows of houses in the country play an even more important role than their urban cousins in the composition of a home. They permit visual access to what for most people is the main reason for acquiring a house in the country: the sight of greenery, for which the window can act as a framing device with the aid of blinds and other decorative accessories. Both these examples (*opposite and right*) are in houses in upstate New York.

In the grand design: these windows (*right*), of Gothic and Islamic inspiration, open on to the gardens of what was originally the country home of a Viennese banker, built at the beginning of the nineteenth century.

Deep-set windows indicate the thickness of the walls in the old houses of the Mediterranean region in two examples from Andalucia (*above left and right*). A more elegant, arched form offers a glimpse of a garden in a house in Provence (*opposite left*). In New York State an early nineteenth-century window with a deep wooden frame illuminates a room decorated in authentic period colours (*opposite right*).

Halfway between the private, secluded world of the interior and the great outdoors beyond, conservatories, terraces, patios and decks provide ideal locations for the social pleasures of eating, drinking and conversation, as well as for the more solitary ones of reflection and contemplation. In the garden room of a house in California, the positioning of a writing table offers its user a direct view of the foliage beyond (*opposite*). A covered deck at the rear of another Californian house (*right*) makes an ideal alfresco dining area with an easily movable table.

223

From the grand to the relatively humble, all the interiors illustrated here make great play of texture and colour in the very different houses they embellish, from opulence in a grand country house in Spain (*above left*) to simple, rustic touches in an Irish cottage (*opposite right*). Neatly stacked logs, clearly intended for the splendid fireplace, bring the outside into a Provençal house (*above right*). In spite of its Italianate appearance, this elaborate wall-painting (*opposite left*) is in a Finnish country house whose original owners were inspired in their decorative schemes by the styles of the great houses of Southern Europe.

The warm and welcoming quality of seasoned wood pervades these restored log cabins in the Adirondack region of New York State (*left and opposite*). The use of unfinished wood is extended even to smaller objects, such as a lamp stand and a waste-paper bin.

Both the structures and the furniture reflect the early life of what is now a luxury hotel catering to New Yorkers who want to get away from it all, continuing a tradition that goes back to the late nineteenth century.

Not grand, but still formal: careful arrangement of wall decoration and furniture is a striking aspect of these two interiors, one in a Mallorcan house (*left above*) and the other in upstate New York (*left below*). The latter is in one of the restored houses in a historic village complex. Although recent, the wall stencilling reproduces designs from the late eighteenth century. Less formal but utterly expressive in its setting, a sunlit dining area in a Provençal house (*opposite*) comes complete with sturdy rustic furniture and an unpaved floor.

Choosing suitable chairs for the country residence is crucial in creating an overall feel for the interior. Sometimes a more elaborate look seems appropriate (*left above and below*), although there is always something to be said for using pieces made by local craftsmen, even if these have been copied from more sophisticated originals or pattern books. These fan-backed chairs (*opposite*), for instance, are of English inspiration but look entirely at home in their Long Island setting.

Preceding pages: In this restored
interior of a former Huguenot house
in New York State the whole room
seems to group around the fireplace,
which is made even more prominent
by the panelling, painted an
authentic eighteenth-century blue
and incorporating shelves for the
display of small objects. Upholstered
furniture of the period adds a note
of opulence.

These pages: A formal surround, made in New York State at roughly the same time as this Long Island house was built in the late eighteenth century, is undoubtedly the centrepoint of this parlour (*opposite*); even the ceiling moulding echoes its design. In a rustic home in the Adirondacks a raised fireplace completes an already warm and comfortable interior (*above*).

This simple interior in a restored house in New York State is undoubtedly rustic, but also exudes an austere elegance (*right*). The fireplace itself is embellished with iron firedogs; ventilated storage space occupies much of the right-hand side of the central feature.

In any household, and particularly in rural interiors, the mantelpiece is one of the most obvious places for the display of small, significant objects, and the chimney breast an almost unavoidable choice for hanging larger ones. Whether in relatively rough settings – here, in central Australia (*above left*) and in a re-created interior in a Canadian folk museum (*above right*) – or in two more finished, formal French country houses (*opposite left* and *right*), such displays of bibelots and paintings bring an even greater significance to the phrase 'hearth and home'.

The light colours of the surrounds of these two fireplaces set against white or near-white walls make them initially less of a commanding feature than some of the examples illustrated on preceding pages. However, the importance of both these fireplaces is emphasized by the objects and wall decorations that surround them.

Especially interesting is the arrangement of found objects in a Californian country house (*opposite*), stark and highly original; meanwhile, an engaging traditionalism distinguishes this Irish interior (*right*).

Even in the simplest country residences (*opposite*), books still do much to furnish a room, especially when interspersed with a variety of objects, works of art and artefacts. A more finished version of the same decorative approach, in a Provençal house, is still engagingly eclectic (*above*). The books look almost haphazardly arranged, while the presence of many other objects, both on the shelves and throughout the rest of the room, transform the space into something of a family museum.

Collecting objects and displaying them are undoubtedly important in the creation and decoration of a pleasing rustic habitat, especially when these collections are from the pre-plastics age and in some way reflect previous practices and usages in the house. Kitchenware and former utilitarian items – crockery, utensils, pots and baskets, for instance – make a splendid sight in the cabinets or on the open shelves of any country kitchen. These antique plates and pots make a variegated display in a corner cupboard in a country house in New York State (*above left*). In a house of Huguenot origin in the same region (*above right*), an eighteenth-century cupboard is crammed with English and American pottery, including mocha earthenware, which was produced in the nineteenth century in England and the United States for taverns and humble homes. A food safe (*opposite left*) in another New York home, built in the mid-eighteenth century by Dutch settlers, contains the owner's collection of baskets. Glasses and usable crockery are stacked neatly in the antique kitchen cupboard of a Provençal house (*opposite right*).

Both decorative and utilitarian, treasured pottery and utensils in everyday use add charm and atmosphere to the country house, introducing elements of display and pattern in the kitchen. Ingeniously positioned racks keep more precious articles out of harm's way in a kitchen in Bohemia (*left above*); wooden spoons and forks, rolling pins and graters – some decorative, others in constant use – are slotted into grooves in a strip of wood (*left below*).

Glassware with a variety of shapes, sizes and intended uses makes a marvellously luminous display against the light streaming through a Provençal kitchen window (*right above*). Collections of wares not intended for use are often displayed outside the kitchen, but a traditional wooden dresser is still one of the most effective ways of showing off a collection of crockery; here a display of nineteenth-century spongeware in an Irish country house (*right below*). This range of pottery, usually produced in Staffordshire, England, was so-called because the vivid colours were applied by sponge through a stencil, creating a slightly blotchy look.

As an end-note to this account of country living, on these and following pages we have picked out a number of details from different houses that seem to sum up much of what makes us value rural life and want to experience something that cannot be found in a large metropolis.

These pages: Home-made jams and preserves from locally grown fruit, stout shoes for walking in the countryside, board games for long winter evenings, and fresh food from the garden – the simple but special pleasures of the countryside.

Overleaf and following pages: Light is a fundamental ingredient in country life, and in the preceding pages we have seen an abundance of table lamps and chandeliers used in place of spotlights and downlights. But candlelight – often the most evocative light of all – should not be overlooked. In older country houses traditional lighting devices still have great ornamental attraction, even if their original utilitarian value is much diminished, as in the case of a mirrored candle (*page 250*), an oil lamp complete with wick and glass funnel (*page 251*) and an array of candlesticks on the parlour mantelpiece in a restored clapboard house in upstate New York (*pages 252–53*).

ACKNOWLEDGMENTS

Cover images © Estate of Gilles de Chabaneix

Designed by Stafford Cliff
Index compiled by Anna Bennett

First published in the United Kingdom in 2008 by
Thames & Hudson Ltd
181A High Holborn
London WC1V 7QX

First paperback edition 2014

The Way We Live: With Colour
© 2008 Thames & Hudson Ltd, London

All photographs
© 2008 Estate of Gilles de Chabaneix

Design and layout
© 2008 Stafford Cliff

Text and captions
© 2008 Thames & Hudson Ltd, London

British Library Cataloguing-in-Publication Data
A catalogue record for this book is available from
the British Library

ISBN 978-0-500-29135-1

Printed and bound in Malaysia by C.S. Graphics

To find out about all our publications, please visit
www.thamesandhudson.com.
There you can subscribe to our e-newsletter,
browse or download our current catalogue,
and buy any titles that are in print.

The photographs in *The Way We Live* series of books are
the result of many years of travelling around the world to
carry out commissions for various publications.
Very special thanks is due to Catherine de Chabaneix, for
all her help during the production of this book, and for her
ongoing commitment to Gilles' remarkable archive.
In addition, thanks to all the people who have helped to
make the realization of this project possible, including
Martine Albertin, Béatrice Amagat, Catherine Ardouin,
Françoise Ayxandri, Marion Bayle, Jean-Pascal Billaud,
Anna Bini, Marie-Claire Blanckaert, Barbara Bourgois,
Marie-France Boyer, Marianne Chedid, Alexandra
D'Arnoux, Jean Demachy, Emmanuel de Toma, Geneviève
Dortignac, Jérôme Dumoulin, Marie-Claude Dumoulin,
Lydia Fiasoli, Jean-Noel Forestier, Marie Kalt, Françoise
Labro, Anne Lefèvre, Hélène Lafforgue, Catherine Laroche,
Nathalie Leffol, Blandine Leroy, Marianne Lohse,
Véronique Méry, Chris O'Byrne, Christine Puech, José
Postic, Nello Renault, Daniel Rozensztroch, Elisabeth Selse,
Suzanne Slesin, Caroline Tiné, Francine Vormèse, Claude
Vuillermet, Suzanne Walker, Rosaria Zucconi and
Martin Bouazis.

Our thanks also go to those who allowed us access to their
houses and apartments: Jean-Marie Amat, Mea Argentieri,
Avril, Claire Basler, Bébèche, Luisa Becaria, Dominique
Bernard, Dorothée Boissier, Carole Bracq, Susie and Mark
Buell, Michel Camus, Laurence Clark, Anita Coppet and
Jean-Jacques Driewir, David Cornell, Bertile Cornet, Jane
Cumberbatch, Geneviève Cuvelier, Ricardo Dalasi, Anne
and Pierre Damour, Catherine Dénoual, Dominique and
Pierre Bénard Dépalle, Phillip Dixon, Ann Dong, Patrice
Doppelt, Philippe Duboy, Christian Duc, Jan Duclos
Maïm, Bernard Dufour, Explora Group, Flemish
Primitives, Michèle Fouks, Pierre Fuger, Massimiliano
Fuksas, Teresa Fung and Teresa Roviras, Henriette
Gaillard, Jean and Isabelle Garçon, John MacGlenaghan,
Fiora Gondolfi, Annick Goutal and Alain Meunier,
Murielle Grateau, Michel and Christine Guérard, Yves and
Michèle Halard, Hotel Le Sénéchal, Hotel Samod Haveli,
Anthony Hudson, Ann Huybens, Patrick T'Hoft, Igor and
Lili, Michèle Iodice, Paul Jacquette, Hellson, Jolie Kelter
and Michael Malcé, Amr Khalil, Dominique Kieffer,

Kiwayu Safari Village, Lawrence and William Kriegel,
Philippe Labro, Karl Lagerfeld, François Lafanour, Nad
Laroche, Rudolph Thomas Leimbacher, Philippe Lévèque
and Claude Terrijn, Marion Lesage, Lizard Island Hotel,
Luna, Catherine Margaretis, Marongiu, Mathias, Valérie
Mazerat and Bernard Ghèzy, Jean-Louis Mennesson, Ilaria
Miani, Anna Moï, Leonardo Mondadori, Jacqueline
Morabito, Christine Moussière, Paola Navone, Christine
Nicaise, Christian Neirynck, Jean Oddes, Catherine Painvin,
John Pawson, Christiane Perrochon, Phong Pfeufer,
Françoise Pialoux les Terrasses, Alberto Pinto, Stéphane
Plassier, Morgan Puett, Bob Ramirez, Riad Dar Amane, Riad
Dar Kawa, Yagura Rié, Guillaume Saalburg, Holly Salomon,
Jérôme-Abel Séguin, Jocelyne and Jean-Louis Sibuet, Siegrid
and her cousins, Valérie Solvi, Tapropane Villa, Patis and
Tito Tesoro, Richard Texier, Jérôme Tisné, Doug Tomkins,
Anna and Patrice Touron, Christian Tortu, Armand Ventilo,
Véronique Vial, Barbara de Vries, Thomas Wegner, Quentin
Wilbaux, Catherine Willis.
Thanks are also due to the following magazines for allowing
us to include photographs originally published by them:
Architectural Digest (French Edition), *Atmosphère, Coté Sud,
Elle, Elle à Table, Elle Décoration, Elle Décor Italie, Madame
Figaro, Maison Française, Marie Claire, Marie Claire Idées,
Marie Claire Maison, The World of Interiors.*